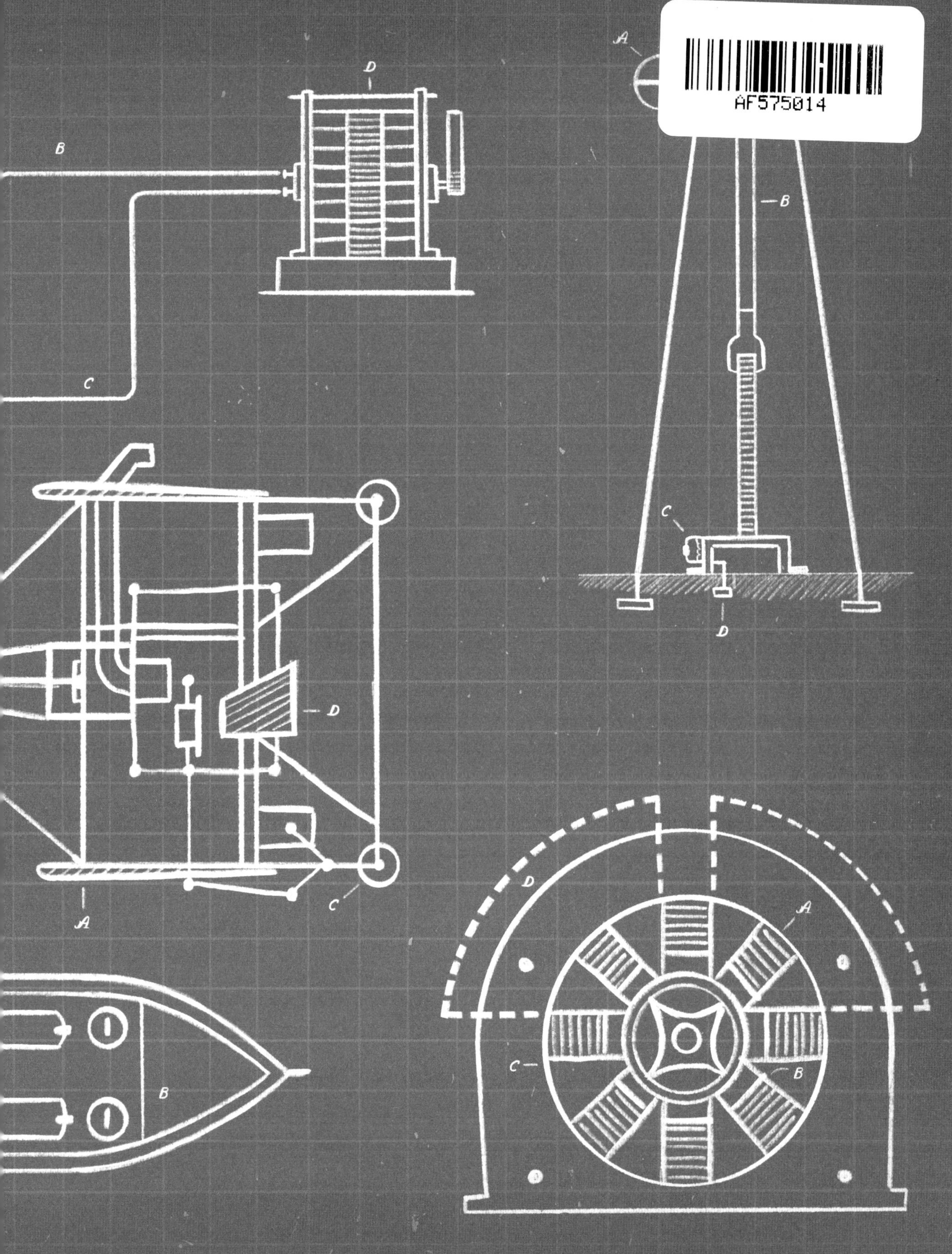

A
D
B
B
C
C
D
D
A
C
D
A
C
B
B

Little People, BIG DREAMS™

NIKOLA TESLA

Written by
Maria Isabel Sánchez Vegara

Illustrated by
Alexander Mostov

Frances Lincoln
Children's Books

This is the story of a Serbian child named Nikola who was born in the middle of a storm. He had three sisters and an older brother. Still, his best friend was Macak, his cat. They lived for each other!

One evening, as he stroked Macak's back, something amazing happened. There were sparks and a crackling noise! His father told Nikola that this natural phenomenon was electricity, the same thing that we see when a lightning bolt strikes a tree.

1+3=4
2×1=2

Discovering the power of electricity made Nikola want to become an inventor. At home, he and his mother loved building small machines and devices. And before he was six, Nikola had created his first motor all by himself.

Soon, Nikola was building his ideas in his imagination. Up there, he designed something, improved it, and even made it go! Once it was ready in his mind, he would create it in real life. And most of the time, it worked.

B
A
D
C
B
A
D
C

In college, Nikola studied electricity under the glow of an oil lamp. At that time, there were no such things as light switches or electrical devices. But he dreamt that one day, the incredible power of electricity would arrive in every home.

He was working on the best way to take electricity from one place to another when the first electric power station opened in London.

It transformed night into day! Still, it had one problem: too much energy was lost when electricity was carried over long distances.

Nikola invented a system that solved that problem! It used an electrical flow called "alternating current." Thanks to it, electricity could be carried far without being wasted. Soon, he was ready to share it with the rest of the world.

He arrived in New York from Paris in 1884, months before the Statue of Liberty. Nikola was recommended for a job with Thomas Edison, the man who had launched the first electric power station and the first light bulbs.

But even though Nikola became his best engineer and hardest worker, Mr Edison didn't believe in alternating current. So Nikola left Edison's company and two years later, he sold his invention to another businessman.

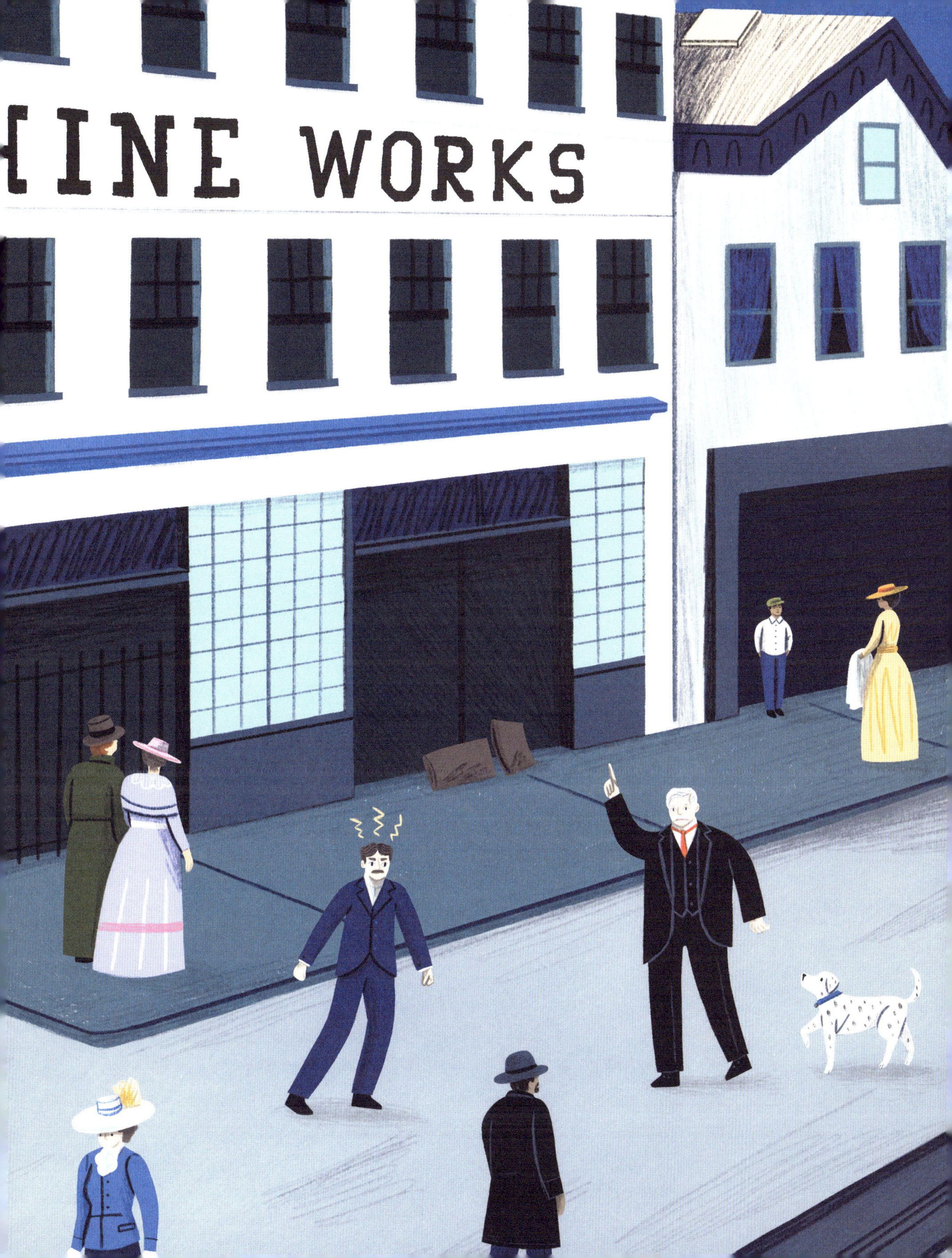
INE WORKS

Soon, 160,000 light bulbs lit up the sky of Chicago thanks to his technology. And three years later, a power station at Niagara Falls brought power all the way to Buffalo, a city in New York. It was the triumph of Nikola's current!

Everybody wanted to meet Nikola and visit his lab, even famous artists and writers like Mark Twain.

He dazzled his scientific peers with shows that looked like magic. Once, to demonstrate one of his inventions, he sent a huge amount of electricity through his body.

Nikola kept thinking of many more helpful devices, from robots to remote controls. He even imagined that—one day—the wind and the sun would give us endless energy and that messages and pictures could be sent wirelessly, too.

And even though the wonders of yesterday are common today, the world still finds inspiration in little Nikola: the genius engineer and tireless inventor who electrified the 20th century and lit up the future.

NIKOLA TESLA

(Born 1856 – Died 1943)

1882

1896

In the village of Smiljan in present-day Croatia, Nikola Tesla came into the world on 10th July 1856. Born during a lightning storm, his mother Djuka proclaimed that her son would be a child of light. His father was a priest of the Eastern Orthodox Church and wanted his son to follow the same path, but Nikola preferred to create homemade inventions with Djuka. He studied engineering in college, dropping out early to begin work as an electrician. Nikola learned about alternating current (AC): a flow of electricity that regularly changes direction. He realized that AC could carry electricity over long distances, meaning that it was more efficient than the system in common use at the time, direct current (DC)—a flow of electricity in one direction. In 1883, he created a motor that harnessed the power

1919

1935

of AC. The following year, Nikola went to America to work with Thomas Edison, who was developing new electrical technology. But six months into his job, Nikola quit after a disagreement between the two; this was the beginning of a life-long rivalry as Edison favored electricity powered by his own DC equipment. Nikola sold the patent for his invention to an electric company, and the AC system won the battle of the currents as the world saw its benefits. Today, electricity from AC is used to power lots of things, such as the electricity for houses. Nikola was a prolific inventor with around 300 patents to his name, including the Tesla coil which is used in electrical equipment such as television sets. He didn't get rich from his creations, but his imagination and creativity changed the world into what it is today.

Want to find out more about **Nikola Tesla?**

Have a read of this great book:

Who Was Nikola Tesla?
by Jim Gigliotti

Brimming with creative inspiration, how-to projects, and useful information to enrich your everyday life, quarto.com is a favorite destination for those pursuing their interests and passions.

First Published in the USA in 2022 by Frances Lincoln Children's Books, an imprint of The Quarto Group.
Quarto Boston North Shore, 100 Cummings Center, Suite 265D, Beverly, MA 01915, USA
Tel: +1 978-282-9590, Fax: +1 978-283-2742 **www.Quarto.com**

A catalogue record for this book is available from the British Library.
ISBN 978-0-7112-7083-1
Set in Futura BT.

Published by Peter Marley • Designed by Lyli Feng
Edited by Lucy Menzies • Production by Nikki Ingram
Editorial Assistance from Rachel Robinson
Manufactured In Guangdong, China CC042022
1 3 5 7 9 8 6 4 2

Photographic acknowledgements (pages 28-29, from left to right): 1.Nikola Tesla (1856-1943), Serb-US physicist and electrical engineer. © Nikola Tesla Museum via Science Photo Library. 2. Serbian-American inventor, engineer and futurist Nikola Tesla (1856 - 1943) aged 40, circa 1896. © ullstein bild Dtl via Getty Images. 3. Nikola Tesla (1856-1943), Serb-US physicist and electrical engineer, holding the gas-filled phosphor-coated 'wireless light bulb' that he had developed in the 1890s. Photographed in around 1919, by the Sarony photographic studio, New York, USA. © Nikola Tesla Museum via Science Photo Library. 4. NIKOLA TESLA (1856-1943). /American electrician, physicist, and inventor. Born in Croatia, of Serbian parents. Photographed in his suite at the Hotel New Yorker in New York City, 1935. © Granger Historical Picture Archive via Alamy Stock Photo.

Collect the *Little People,* **BIG DREAMS**™ series:

FRIDA KAHLO

COCO CHANEL

MAYA ANGELOU

AMELIA EARHART

AGATHA CHRISTIE

MARIE CURIE

ROSA PARKS

AUDREY HEPBURN

EMMELINE PANKHURST

ELLA FITZGERALD

ADA LOVELACE

JANE AUSTEN

GEORGIA O'KEEFFE

HARRIET TUBMAN

ANNE FRANK

MOTHER TERESA

JOSEPHINE BAKER

L. M. MONTGOMERY

JANE GOODALL

SIMONE DE BEAUVOIR

MUHAMMAD ALI

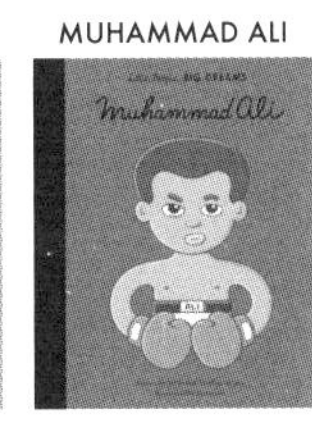

STEPHEN HAWKING

MARIA MONTESSORI

VIVIENNE WESTWOOD

MAHATMA GANDHI

DAVID BOWIE

WILMA RUDOLPH

DOLLY PARTON

BRUCE LEE

RUDOLF NUREYEV

ZAHA HADID

MARY SHELLEY

MARTIN LUTHER KING JR.

DAVID ATTENBOROUGH

ASTRID LINDGREN

EVONNE GOOLAGONG

BOB DYLAN

ALAN TURING

BILLIE JEAN KING

GRETA THUNBERG

JESSE OWENS

JEAN-MICHEL BASQUIAT

ARETHA FRANKLIN

CORAZON AQUINO

PELÉ

ERNEST SHACKLETON

STEVE JOBS

AYRTON SENNA

LOUISE BOURGEOIS

ELTON JOHN

JOHN LENNON

PRINCE

CHARLES DARWIN

CAPTAIN TOM MOORE

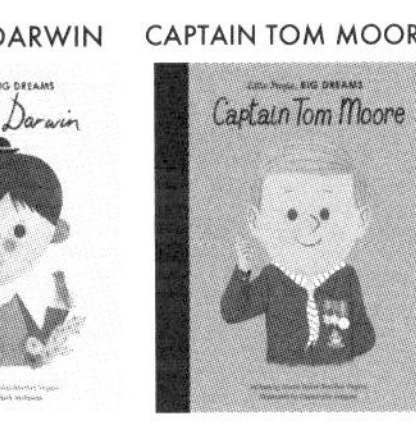

HANS CHRISTIAN ANDERSEN

STEVIE WONDER

MEGAN RAPINOE

MARY ANNING

MALALA YOUSAFZAI

ANDY WARHOL

RUPAUL

MICHELLE OBAMA

MINDY KALING

IRIS APFEL

ROSALIND FRANKLIN

RUTH BADER GINSBURG

MARILYN MONROE

KAMALA HARRIS

ALBERT EINSTEIN

CHARLES DICKENS

YOKO ONO

MICHAEL JORDAN

NELSON MANDELA

PABLO PICASSO

AMANDA GORMAN

GLORIA STEINEM

FLORENCE NIGHTINGALE

HARRY HOUDINI

J.R.R. TOLKIEN

ELVIS PRESLEY

NEIL ARMSTRONG

ALEXANDER VON HUMBOLDT

NIKOLA TESLA

WILMA MANKILLER

ACTIVITY BOOKS

STICKER ACTIVITY BOOK

COLORING BOOK

LITTLE ME, BIG DREAMS JOURNAL

Discover more about the series at www.littlepeoplebigdreams.com

B
A
D
C
A
B
D
A
C
B
A
C
B
D
A